ARE THERE STARS CLOSE TO EARTH?

ASTRONOMY FOR 9 YEAR OLDS CHILDREN'S ASTRONOMY BOOKS

Speedy Publishing LLC

40 E. Main St. #1156

Newark, DE 19711

www.speedypublishing.com

Copyright 2017

Stand outside on a clear night and look up: you are looking across the void of space at stars that are billions of miles away. What are the closest stars to Earth, and what are they like? Let's find out.

TINY SPECKS OF LIGHT

Most of the universe seems to be empty space, possibly filled with "dark matter" that we do not yet understand and can only guess at. But in the vast darkness we look through in the night sky, we see twinkling lights.

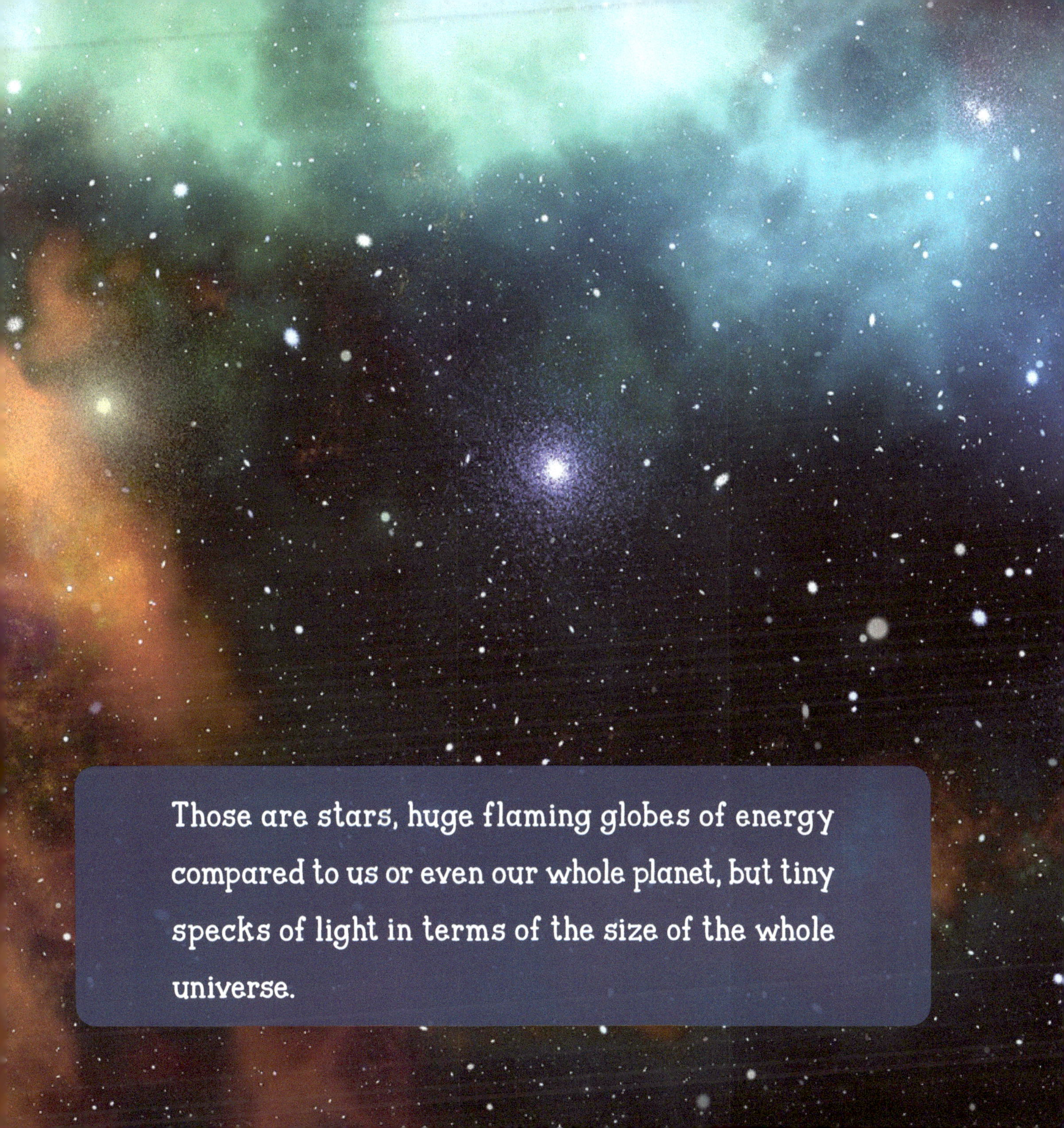
Those are stars, huge flaming globes of energy
compared to us or even our whole planet, but tiny
specks of light in terms of the size of the whole
universe.

Our solar system is out in a spiral arm of a galaxy we call the Milky Way. Here the stars are very far apart. But even toward the center of the galaxy, which is tightly packed in comparison to our neighborhood, the distances are immense.

ILLUSTRATION OF THE MILKY WAY

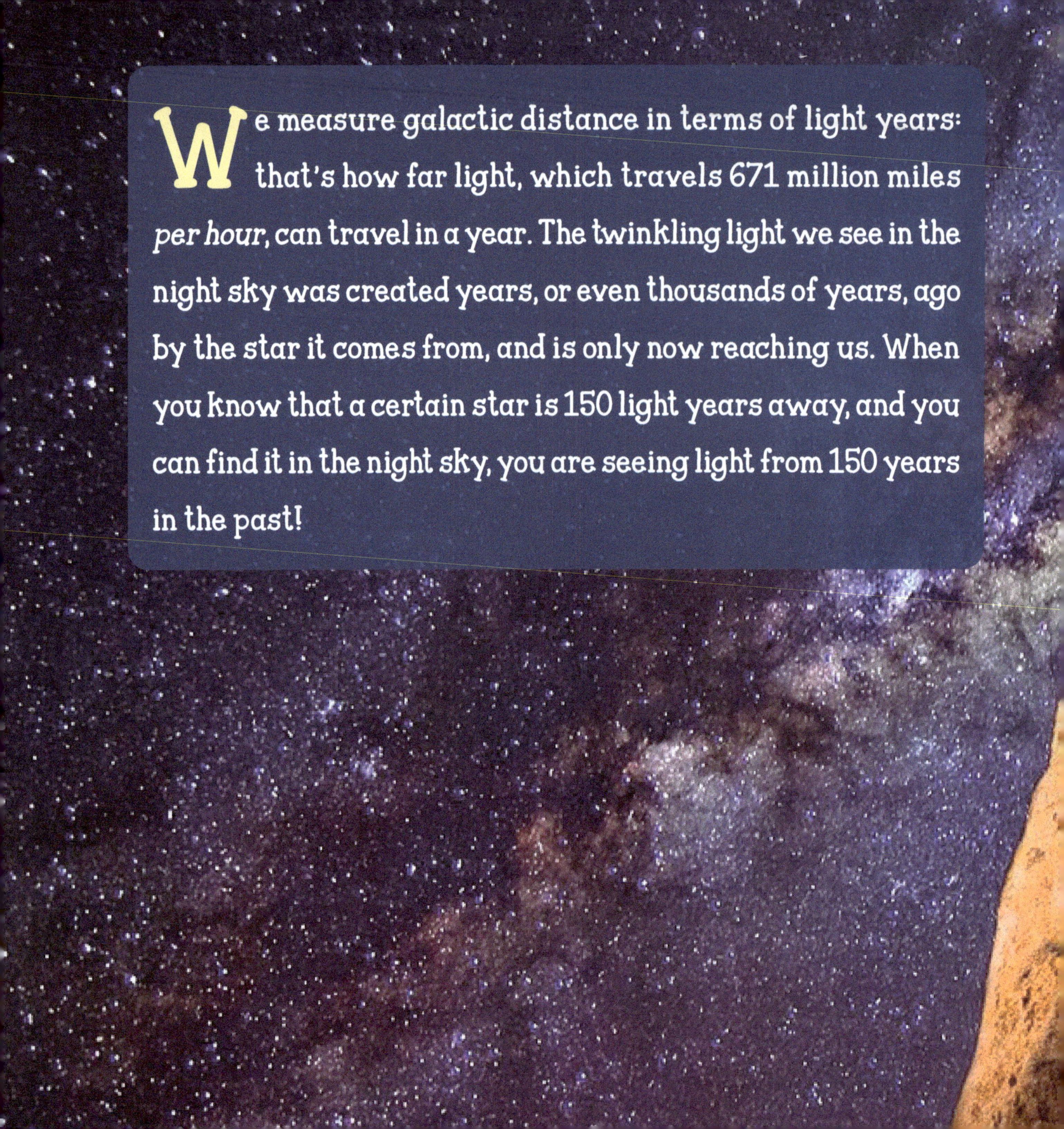
We measure galactic distance in terms of light years: that's how far light, which travels 671 million miles *per hour*, can travel in a year. The twinkling light we see in the night sky was created years, or even thousands of years, ago by the star it comes from, and is only now reaching us. When you know that a certain star is 150 light years away, and you can find it in the night sky, you are seeing light from 150 years in the past!

MILKY WAY

THE SUN IN SPACE

But there is one star that is much closer to us than any other, a star that gives us warmth and lights our every day: the Sun!

OUR SUN

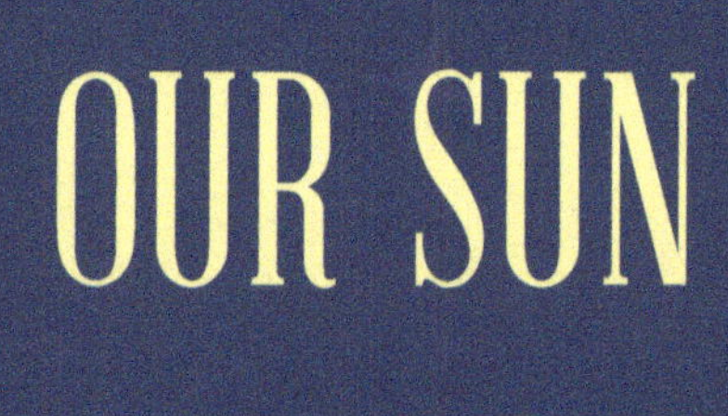

Our Sun is so close to Earth that its light reaches us in only eight minutes! Without the light and warmth the Sun generates, there would be no life on our planet at all.

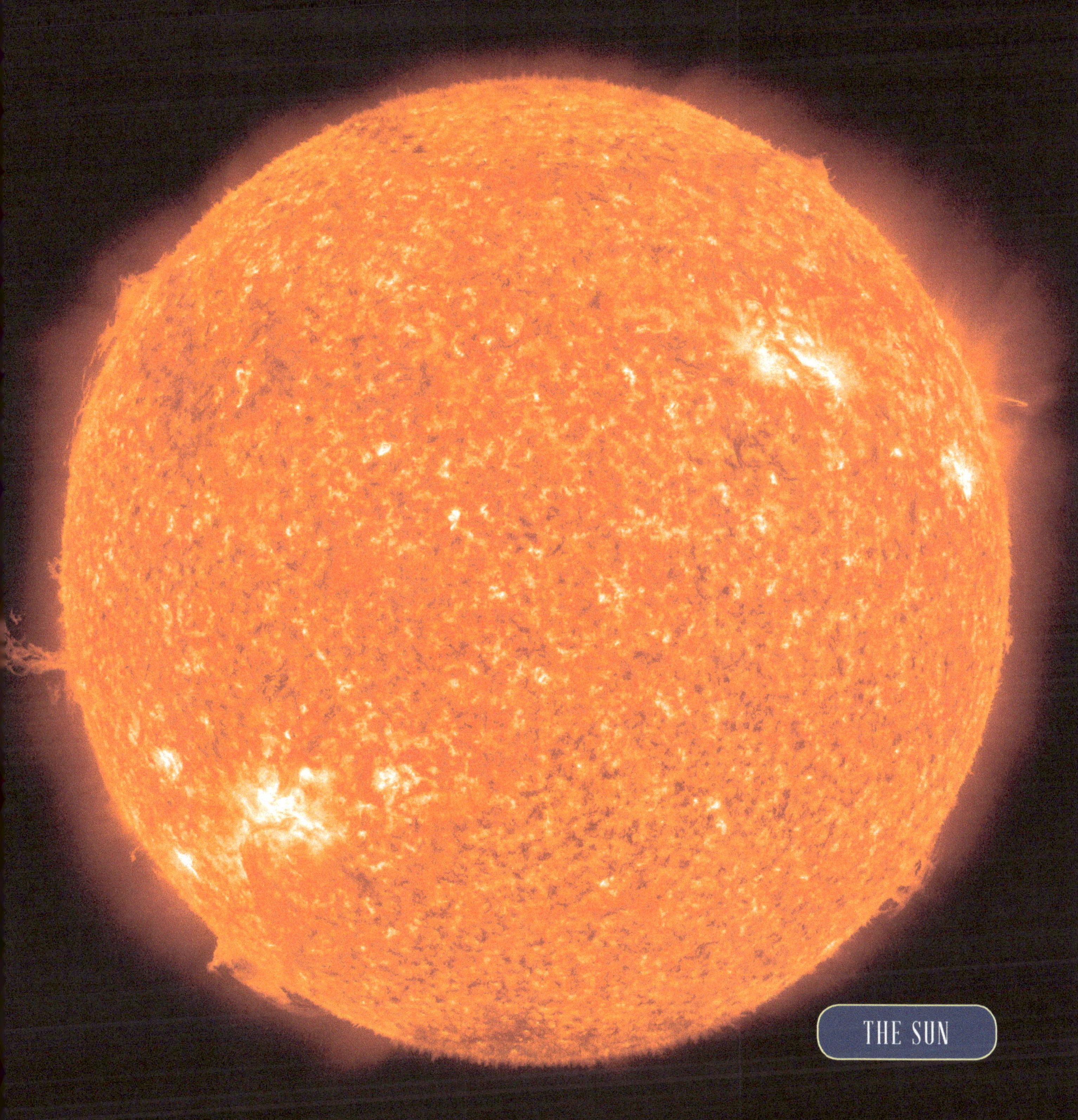
THE SUN

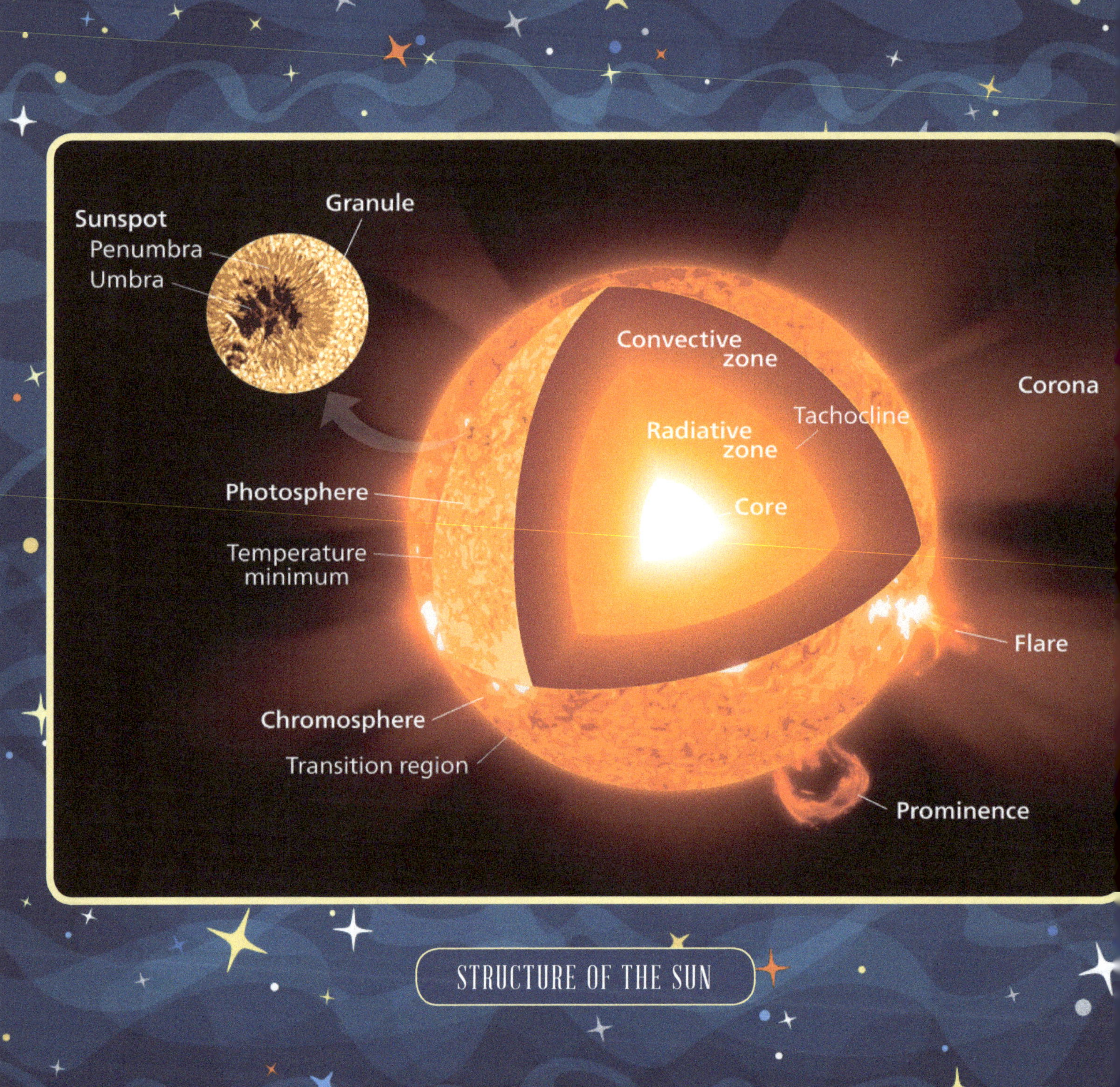

Sunspot
Penumbra
Umbra
Granule
Convective zone
Radiative zone
Tachocline
Corona
Core
Photosphere
Temperature minimum
Flare
Chromosphere
Transition region
Prominence
STRUCTURE OF THE SUN

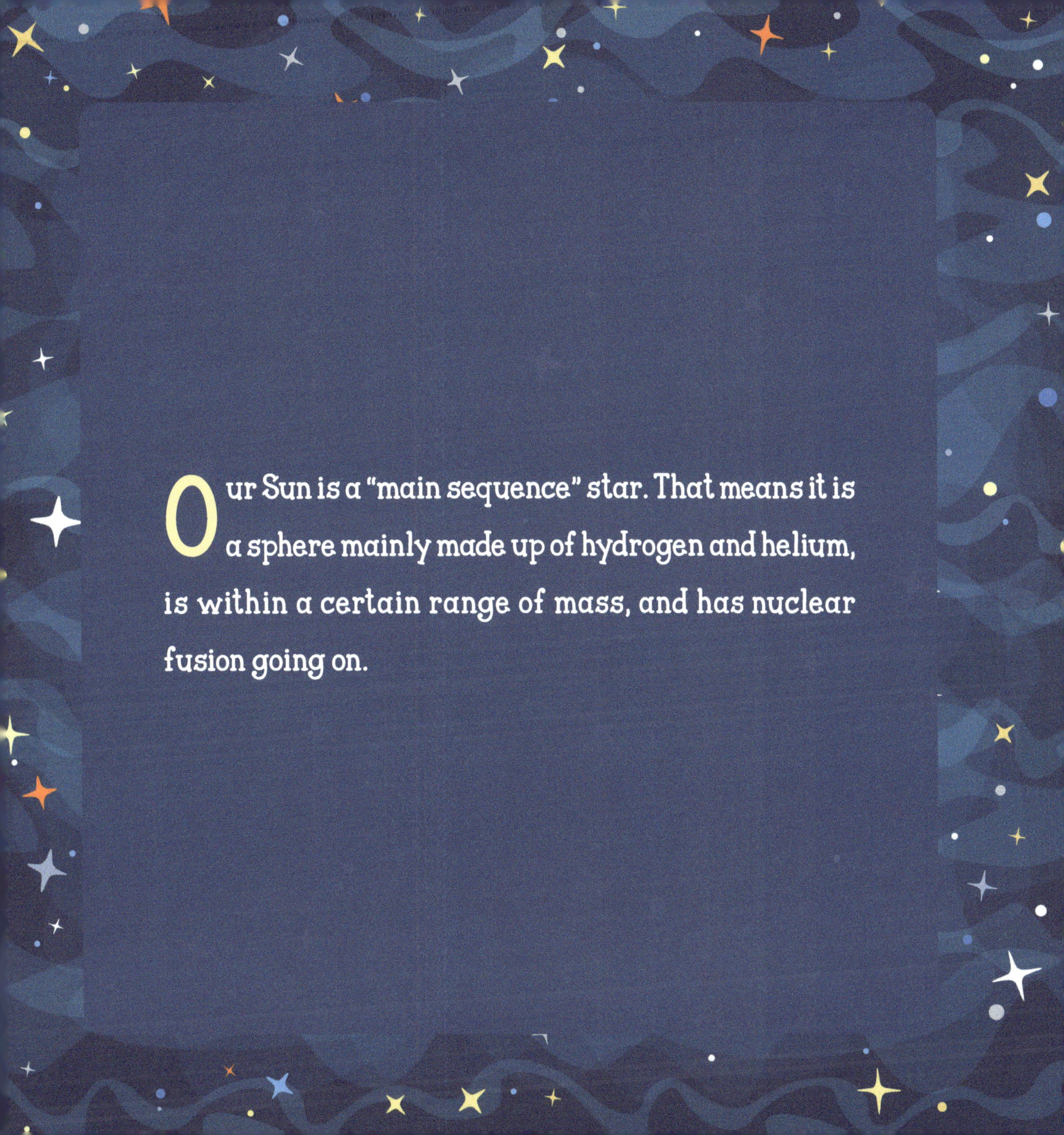

Our Sun is a "main sequence" star. That means it is a sphere mainly made up of hydrogen and helium, is within a certain range of mass, and has nuclear fusion going on.

Nuclear fusion is atoms of one or more lighter elements fusing together to make a heavier element. In our Sun, the lighter element is hydrogen, and hydrogen atoms fuse together to make helium. In the process they release a huge amount of energy, generating heat and light—lots of it!

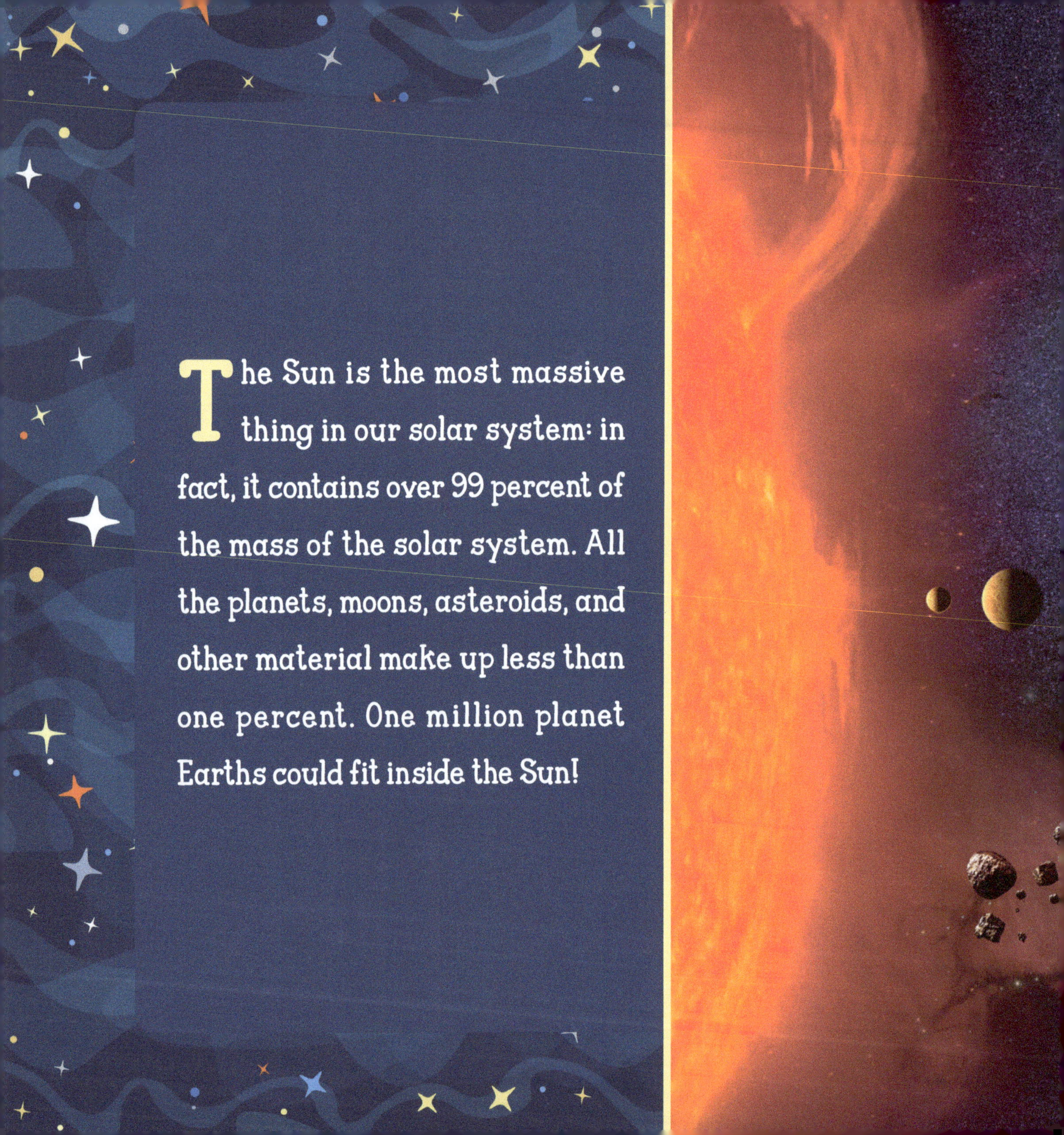

The Sun is the most massive thing in our solar system: in fact, it contains over 99 percent of the mass of the solar system. All the planets, moons, asteroids, and other material make up less than one percent. One million planet Earths could fit inside the Sun!

SOLAR SYSTEM

SOLAR SYSTEM

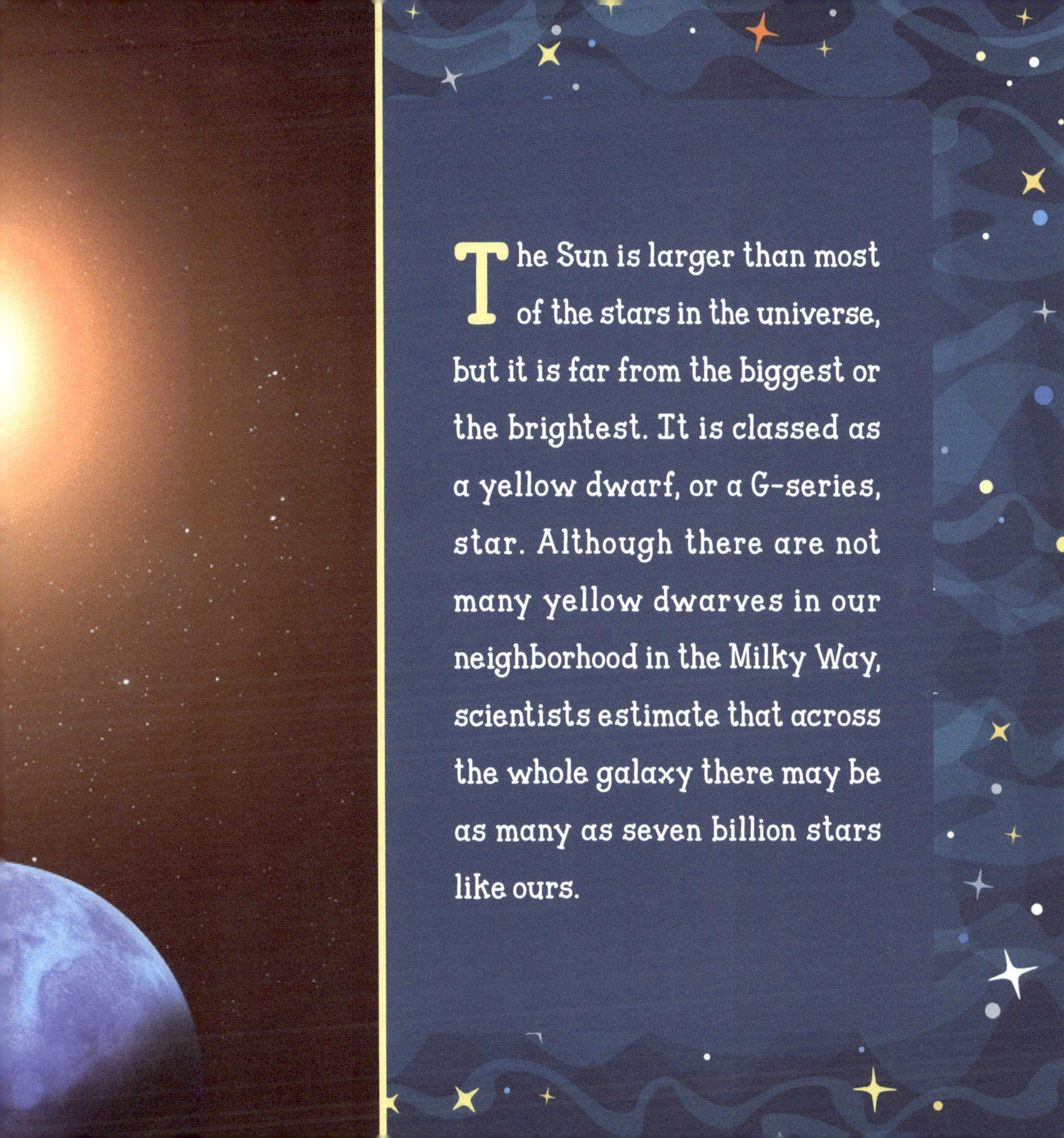

The Sun is larger than most of the stars in the universe, but it is far from the biggest or the brightest. It is classed as a yellow dwarf, or a G-series, star. Although there are not many yellow dwarves in our neighborhood in the Milky Way, scientists estimate that across the whole galaxy there may be as many as seven billion stars like ours.

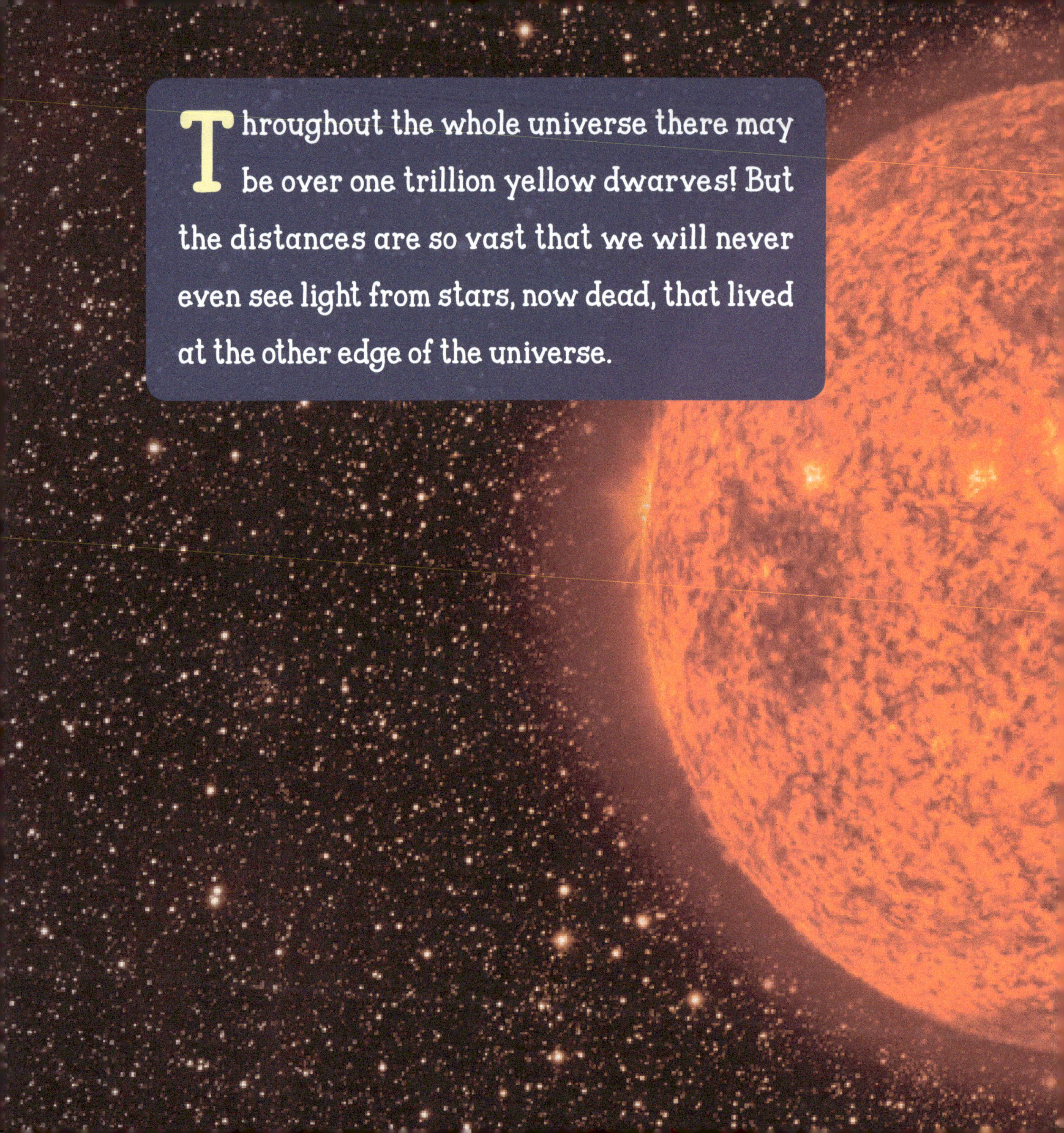

Throughout the whole universe there may be over one trillion yellow dwarves! But the distances are so vast that we will never even see light from stars, now dead, that lived at the other edge of the universe.

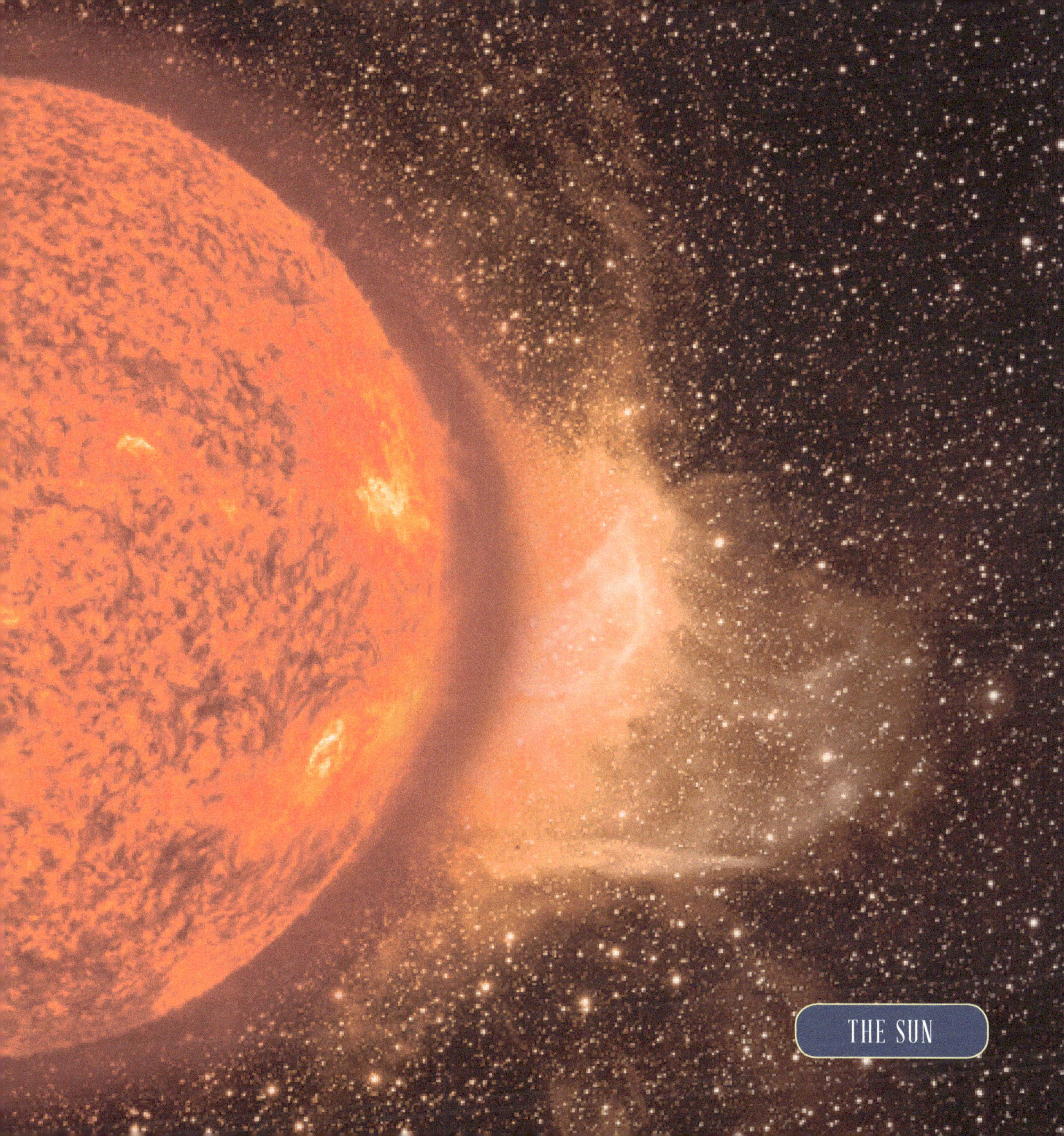
THE SUN

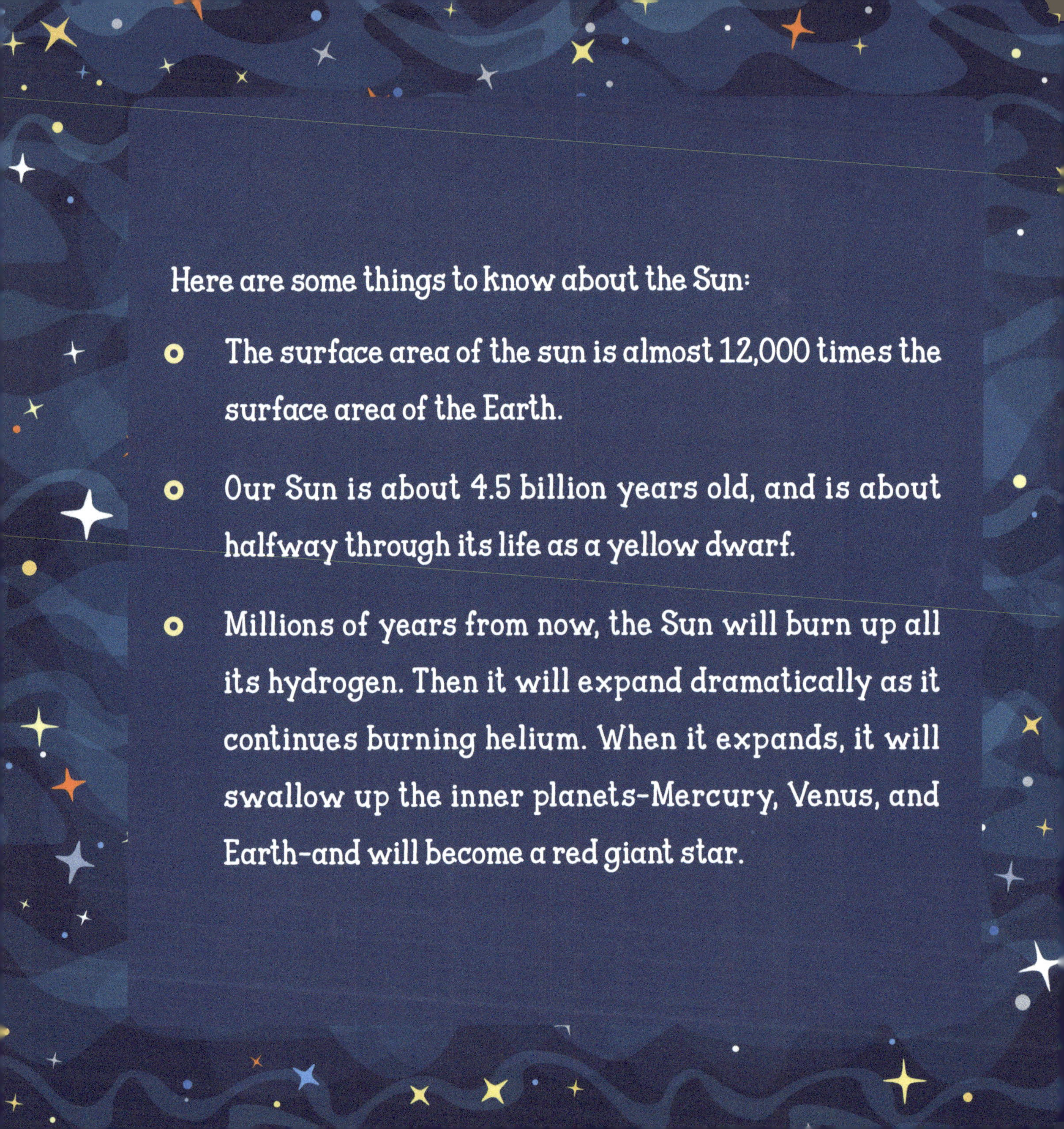

Here are some things to know about the Sun:

- The surface area of the sun is almost 12,000 times the surface area of the Earth.

- Our Sun is about 4.5 billion years old, and is about halfway through its life as a yellow dwarf.

- Millions of years from now, the Sun will burn up all its hydrogen. Then it will expand dramatically as it continues burning helium. When it expands, it will swallow up the inner planets-Mercury, Venus, and Earth-and will become a red giant star.

AN ILLUSTRATION OF SUN'S EXPLOSION

A WHITE DWARF

Long after the Sun becomes a red giant, it will collapse and become a white dwarf. It will have almost the same mass, but compressed together into a sphere smaller than our Earth!

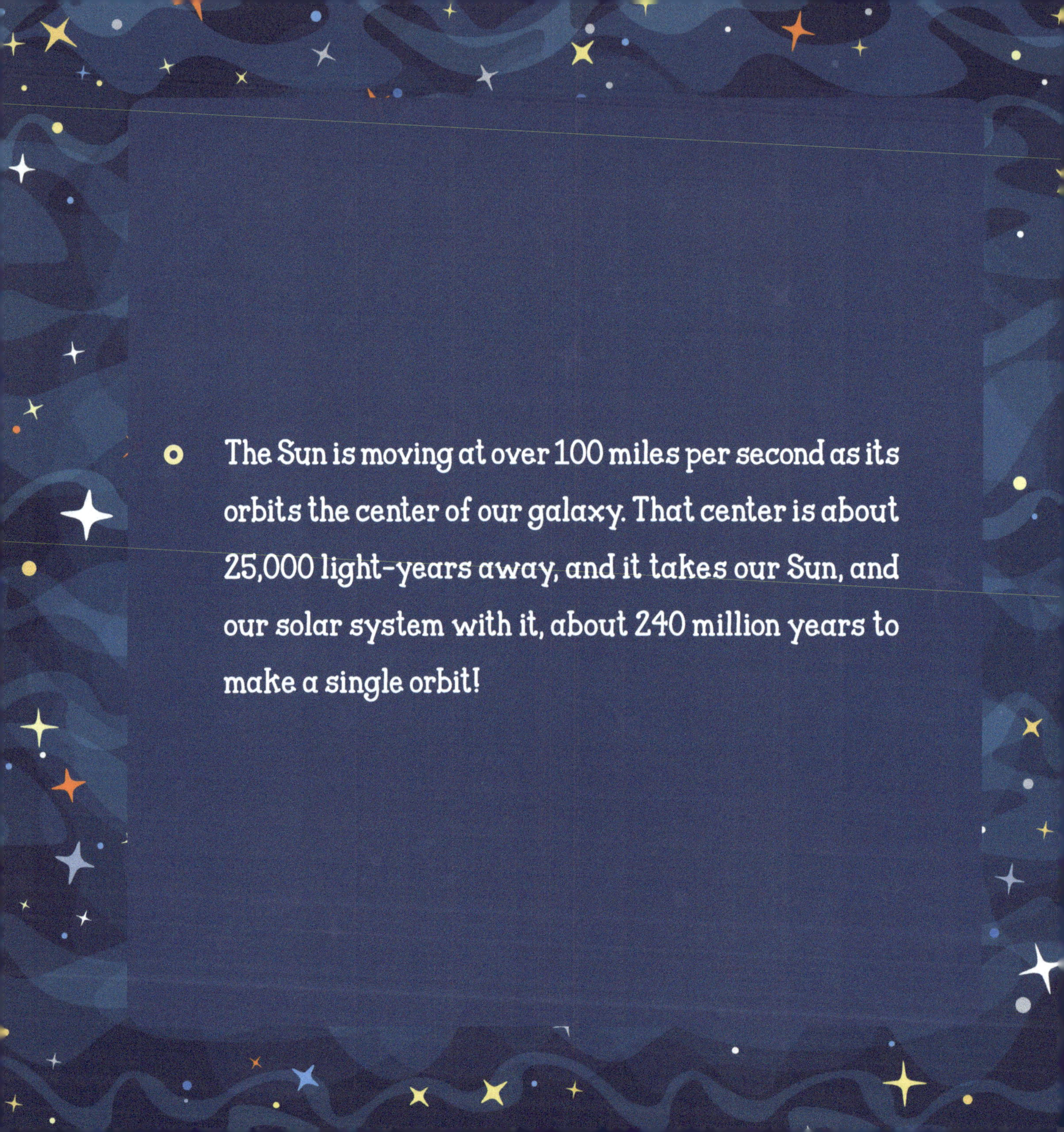

The Sun is moving at over 100 miles per second as its orbits the center of our galaxy. That center is about 25,000 light-years away, and it takes our Sun, and our solar system with it, about 240 million years to make a single orbit!

SOLAR SYSTEM

SOLAR SYSTEM

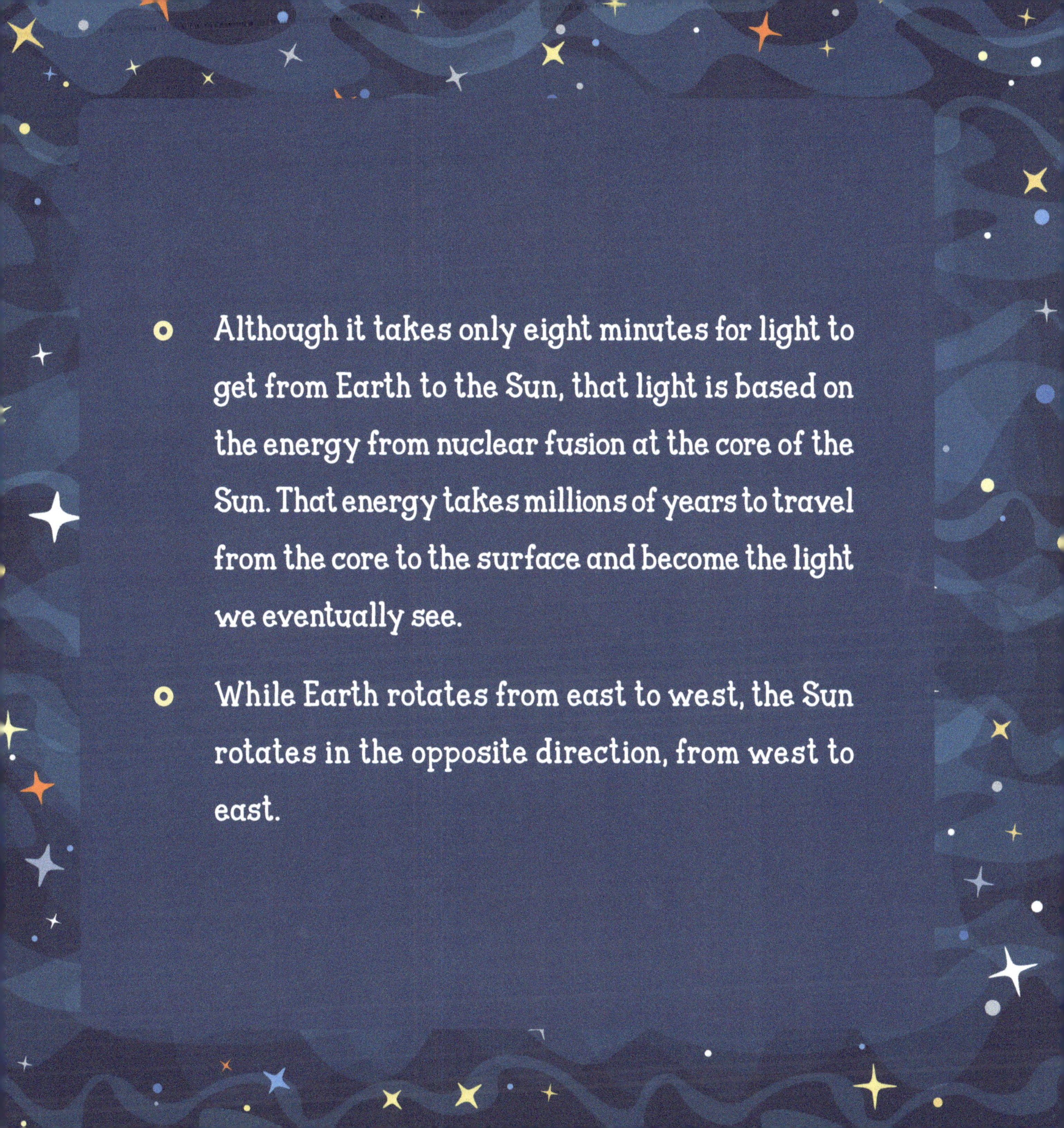

- Although it takes only eight minutes for light to get from Earth to the Sun, that light is based on the energy from nuclear fusion at the core of the Sun. That energy takes millions of years to travel from the core to the surface and become the light we eventually see.

- While Earth rotates from east to west, the Sun rotates in the opposite direction, from west to east.

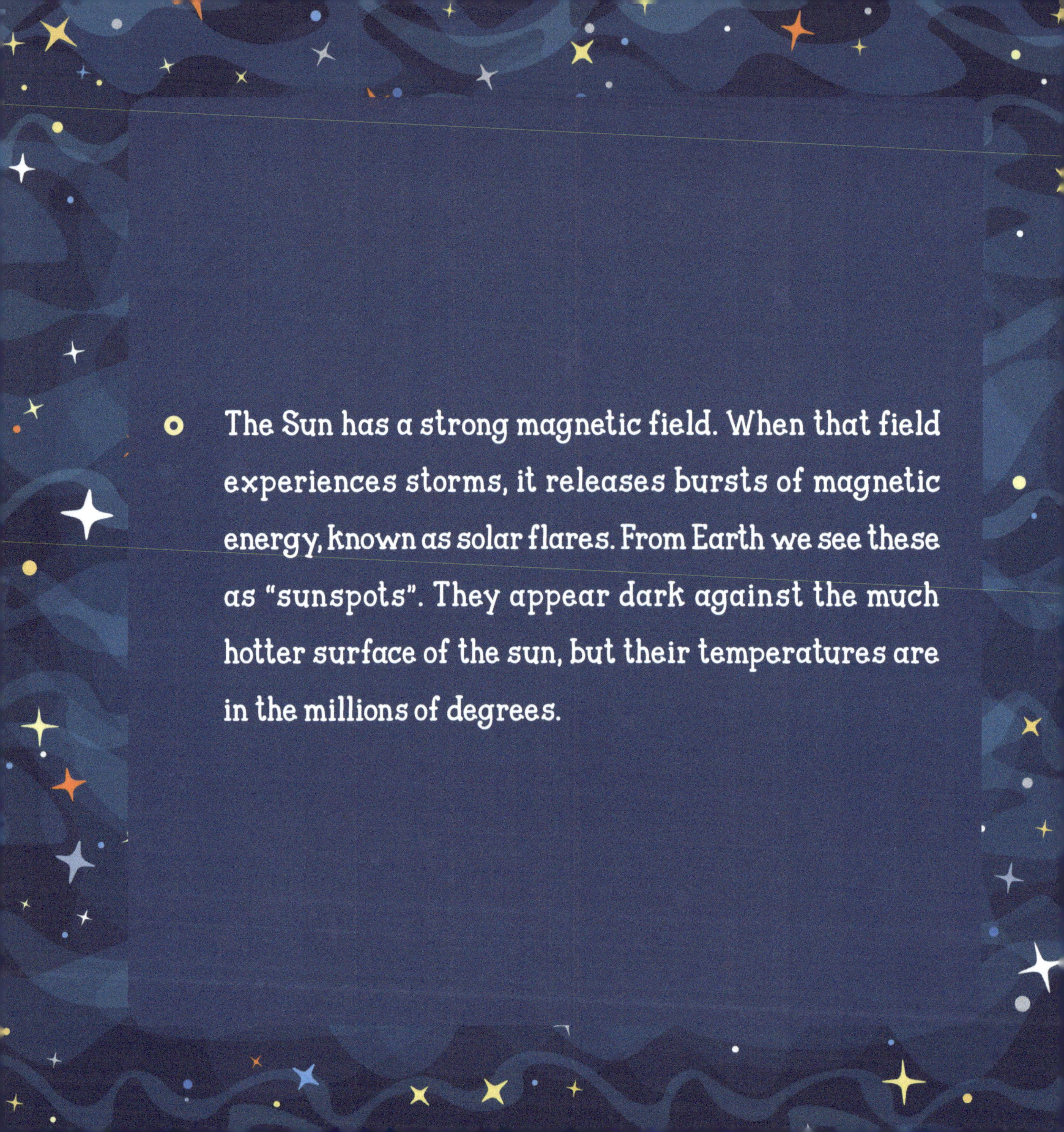
The Sun has a strong magnetic field. When that field experiences storms, it releases bursts of magnetic energy, known as solar flares. From Earth we see these as "sunspots". They appear dark against the much hotter surface of the sun, but their temperatures are in the millions of degrees.

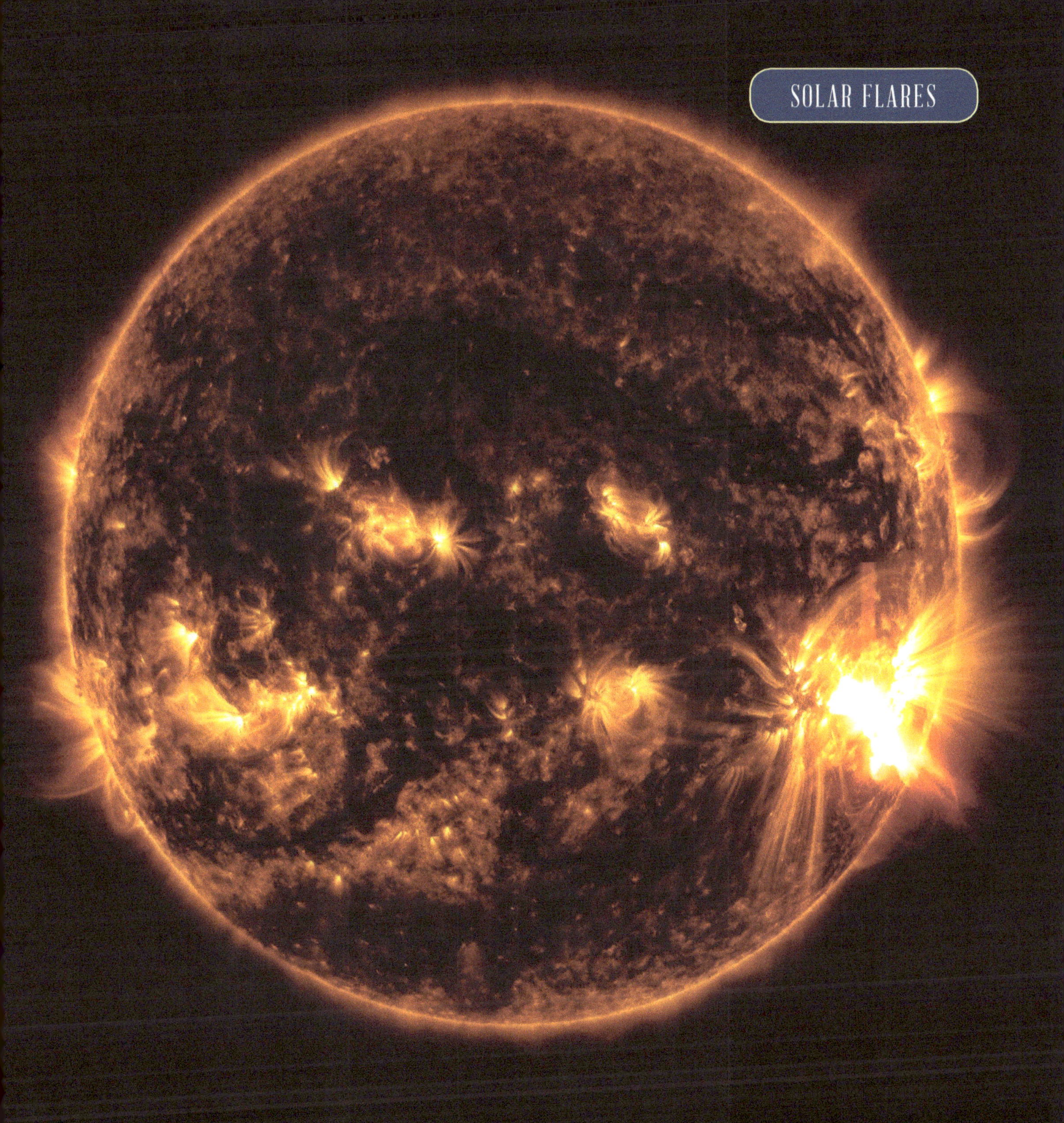
SOLAR FLARES

STARS NEARBY

Our star is immense compared to us, and we could spend a lot of time just concentrating on it. But we have interesting neighbors not all that far way...if you can travel at the speed of light!

Here are some of our neighbors in the galaxy:

Alpha Centauri

This is a triple-star system just over four light-years away. One of the three, Alpha Centauri A, is a type-G star, like our Sun. The other two are red dwarf stars, one of the common star types.

Barnard's Star

This is a red dwarf just under six light-years away. It has the greatest "proper motion" of any star we have found so far. This means it moves more rapidly compared to the stars in its background than any other of our near neighbors.

BARNARD'S STAR 1991
BARNARD'S STAR 2014

Sirius A

Sirius is the brightest star we see at night, because at 8.6 light years away it is relatively close to us and because it is burning very brightly. It is a white dwarf: it is smaller than our Earth, but it has almost the same mass as our Sun.

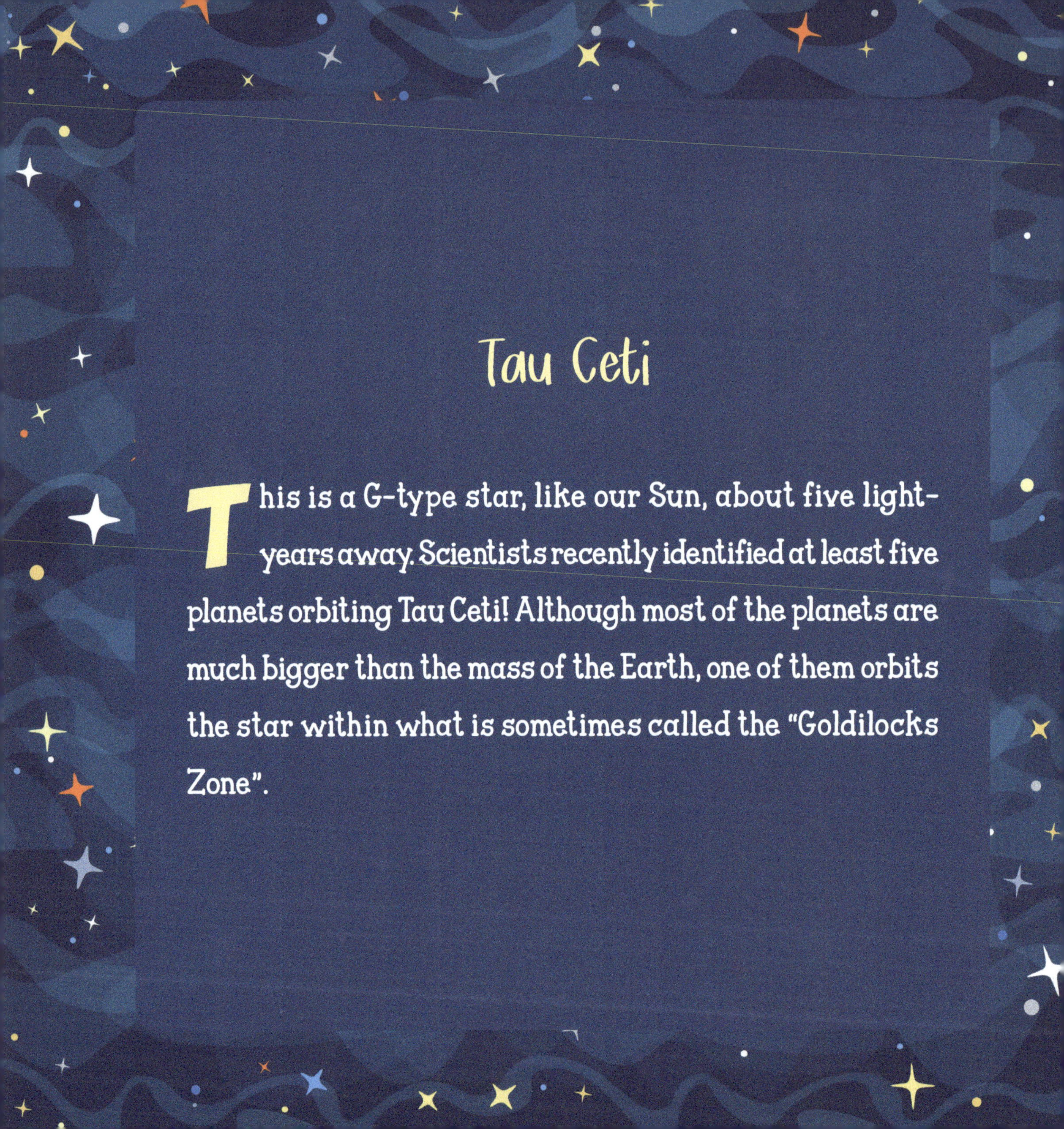

Tau Ceti

This is a G-type star, like our Sun, about five light-years away. Scientists recently identified at least five planets orbiting Tau Ceti! Although most of the planets are much bigger than the mass of the Earth, one of them orbits the star within what is sometimes called the "Goldilocks Zone".

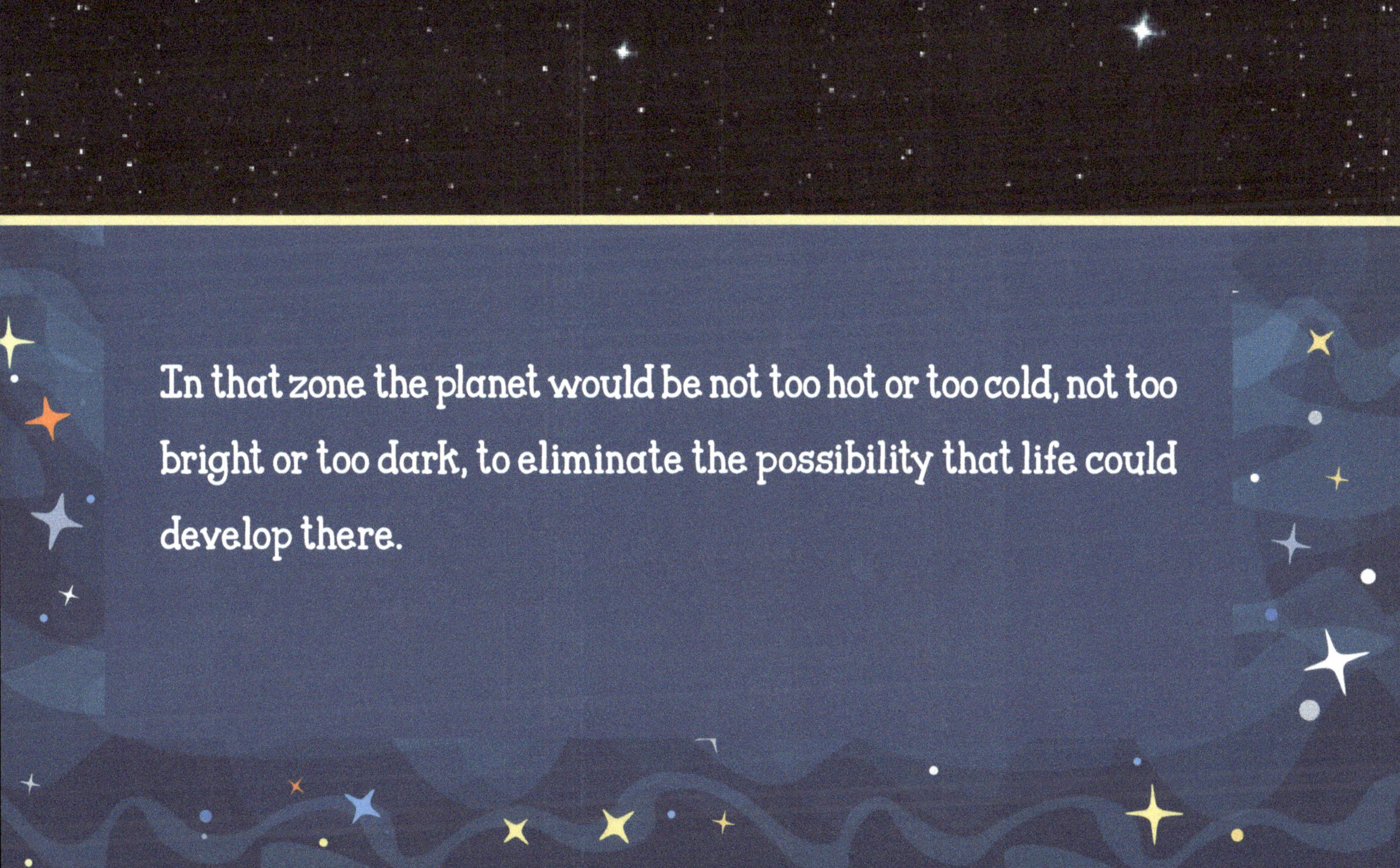
In that zone the planet would be not too hot or too cold, not too bright or too dark, to eliminate the possibility that life could develop there.

The Goldilocks Zone for each star is different, depending on the energy and light the star is giving out. For our solar system Venus, the Earth, and Mars are all within our Sun's Goldilocks Zone. (Some moons further out in our solar system also have the possibility of supporting life of some sort: read the Baby Professor book *Is our Moon the Only Moon in the Solar System?* to learn more.)

Wolf 359

Wolf 359 is less than eight light-years from Earth, but because it is a dim reddish star you cannot see it without a telescope. Wolf 359's claim to fame is that it is the location of a huge battle in the TV series *Star Trek: The Next Generation* between the Federation (including us humans) and a powerful enemy called the Borg.

Lalande 21185

This star is in the Big Dipper, the constellation Ursa Major, but it is a faint red dwarf that you cannot see without a telescope. Astronomers think the star may have some planets orbiting it. Lalande is a bit over eight light-years away.

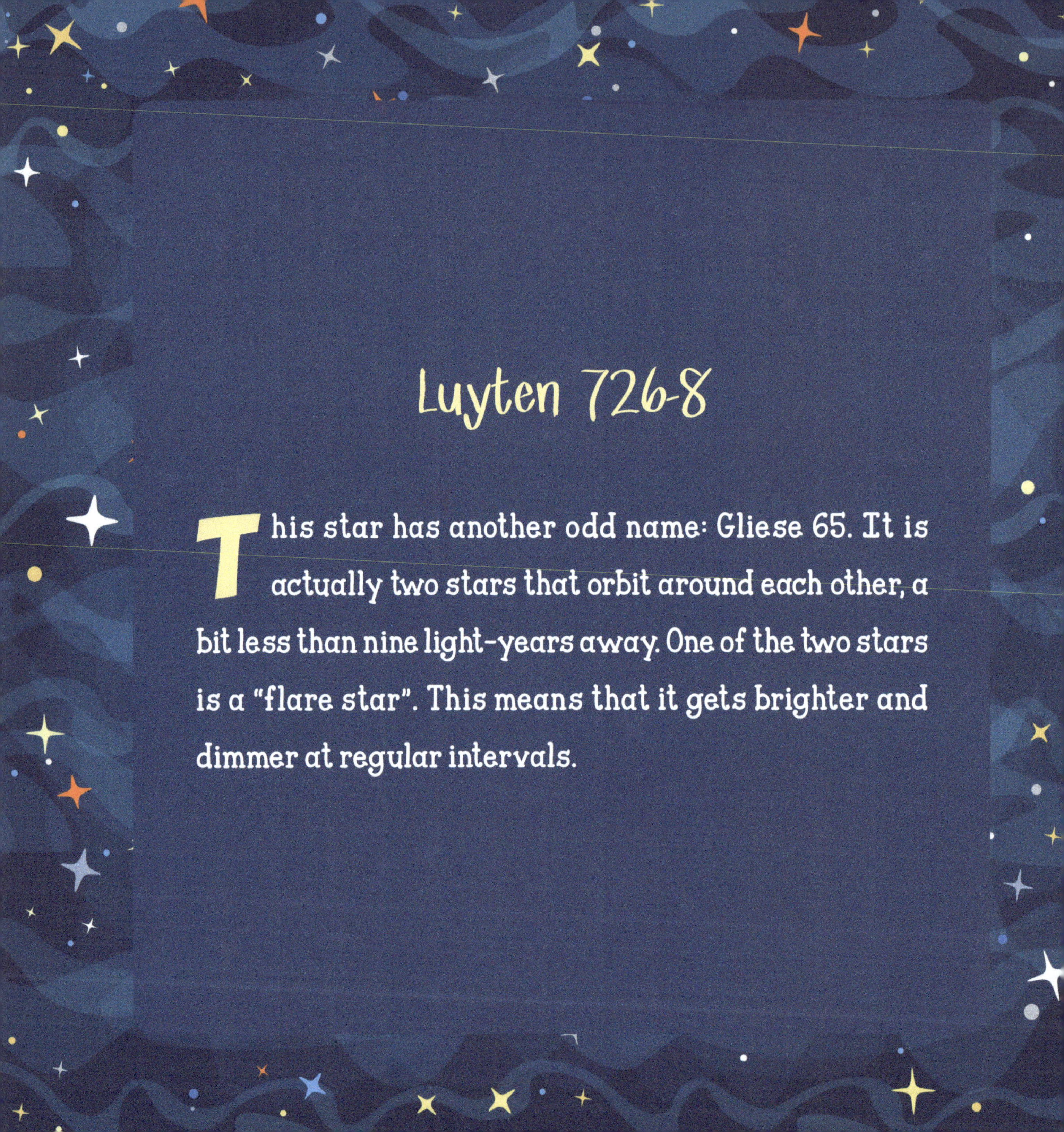

Luyten 726-8

This star has another odd name: Gliese 65. It is actually two stars that orbit around each other, a bit less than nine light-years away. One of the two stars is a "flare star". This means that it gets brighter and dimmer at regular intervals.

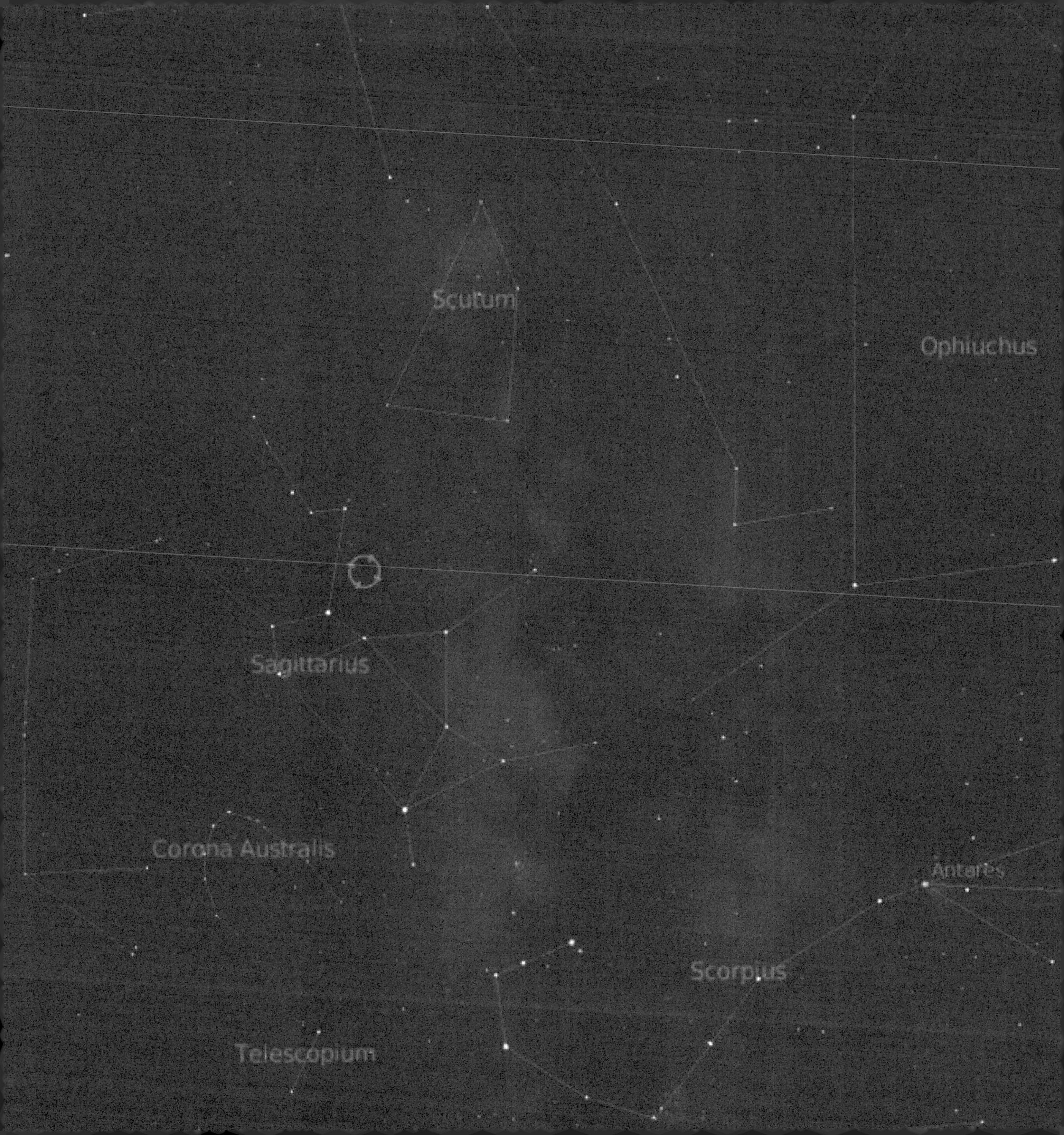

Scutum
Ophiuchus
Sagittarius
Corona Australis
Antares
Scorpius
Telescopium

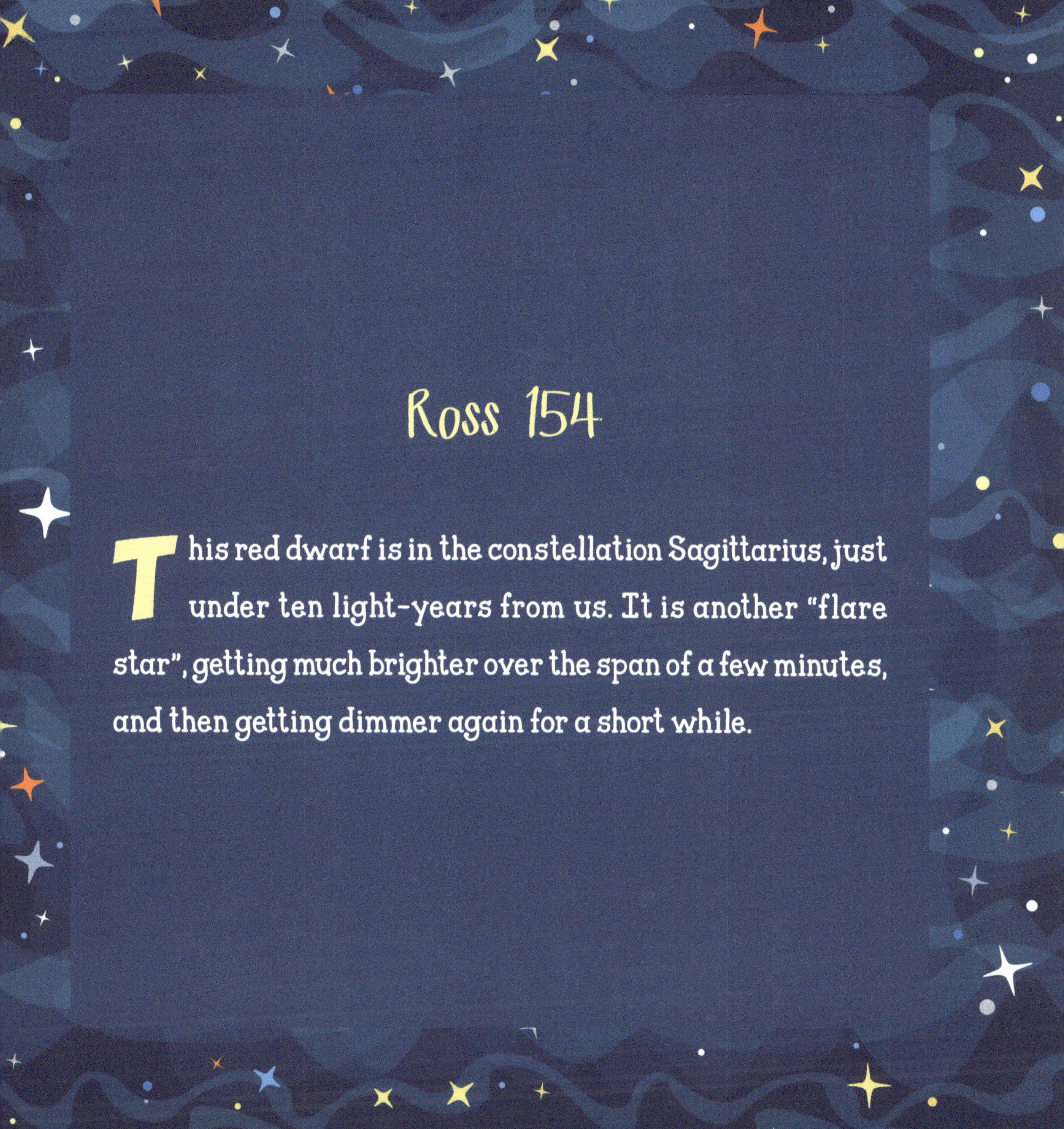

Ross 154

This red dwarf is in the constellation Sagittarius, just under ten light-years from us. It is another "flare star", getting much brighter over the span of a few minutes, and then getting dimmer again for a short while.

Ross 248

This star is right now just over ten light-years from Earth. But it is moving so quickly relative to the orbit of our solar system around the center of the Milky Way galaxy that in 36,000 years (no time at all!) it will be the nearest neighbor to the Sun. However, it will continue zooming past and will no longer be the next-closest star to us only 9,000 years after that.

A PLANET CIRCLING AROUND ROSS 248

EPSILON ERIDANI (IN YELLOW)

Epsilon Eridani

Epsilon Eridani, 10.5 light-years from us, probably has at least two planets orbiting it. It is the third-closest star that we can see with the naked eye.

BOUND FOR SPACE?

Even while we stand still right here on Earth, our planet is carrying us quickly through the universe. The Earth orbits the Sun, the Sun and our whole solar system orbit the center of the Milky Way galaxy, and the whole galaxy is in motion—toward what we do not know.

Find out more about space, and exploration, in Baby Professor books like *Sally Ride: First American Woman in Space*, *What is an Astronaut?* and *A Space Ride to Saturn*.

Visit

www.BabyProfessorBooks.com

to download Free Baby Professor eBooks
and view our catalog of new and exciting
Children's Books